Turtle is a Hero

by Gabby Pritchard
illustrated by Fabrizio di Baldo

 CAMBRIDGE
UNIVERSITY PRESS

 UCL
Institute of Education

Every day, Turtle swam in the deep green sea. He loved to dive and play in the rocks at the bottom of the sea.

One sunny day, Turtle swam all the way to the beach.

The beach was very hot. Turtle found a cool place in the golden sand and made a hole.

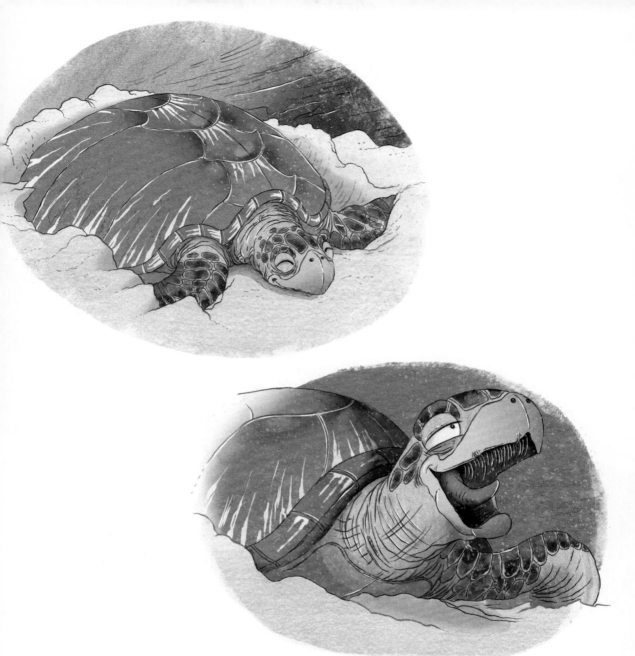

'Perfect,' he said.
Then he yawned and closed his eyes.

Suddenly, Turtle felt a tap on his head.
He opened one eye.

'Hello, little boy,' he said.

'Wow!' gasped the boy. 'You can speak?'

'Of course,' said Turtle. 'Are you afraid?'

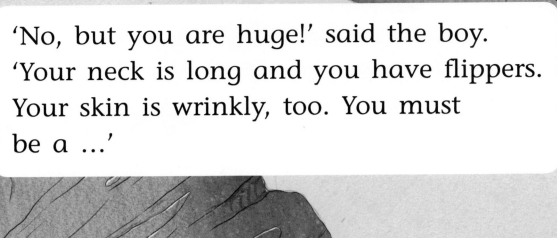

'No, but you are huge!' said the boy.
'Your neck is long and you have flippers.
Your skin is wrinkly, too. You must
be a ...'

Turtle laughed. 'I'm not a dinosaur,'
he said. 'My flippers help me swim fast
... this shell makes me strong ...'

... and your skin would be wrinkly too
if you lived in the sea.'

The boy laughed.
'Yes,' he said.
'I would look just
like an old man.'

The boy touched Turtle's shell. 'I think your shell could be very useful,' he said.

'Come and swim with us,' shouted the boy's friends. The boy waved goodbye and went to play with his friends.

Turtle smiled and began to swim home.

12

Suddenly, he heard the boy shout.
'HELP!' he cried. 'HELP ME!'

The boy was in the sea!
A big wave was coming.

'Hold on,' shouted Turtle.

Turtle swam fast. His flippers helped him race through the sea.

He dived deep ...

and then ...

... up he POPPED.

The boy was sitting
on Turtle's strong shell.

'You saved me!' cried the boy. 'Turtle is a hero!'

Turtle smiled. 'I am not a hero,' he said. 'But I am your friend.'

The boy hugged Turtle. 'I'm so happy that you are my friend,' he said.

Turtle is a Hero — Gabby Pritchard

Teaching notes written by Sue Bodman and Glen Franklin

Using this book

Developing reading comprehension

This story has elements of an often-used idea of a little and seemingly weak creature helping a bigger creature. Initially the little boy only sees the differences between himself and the turtle. They become friends and the turtle is able to save the boy when he gets into difficulty in the sea.

In order to understand why the turtle should help the little boy, some inferences about character need to be gained. Discussions about why the little boy is initially wary and why the turtle is not would be useful in gaining the full meaning of the story.

Grammar and sentence structure

- Use of descriptive language; 'golden sand', 'strong shell', 'deep, green sea', 'cool place'.

Word meaning and spelling

- Challenging vocabulary in this context; 'wrinkly'.
- Reinforce different ways of writing /ee/ words in context: 'deep, green sea'; 'beach'.

Curriculum links

Social Studies – This story could link to a topic of *People who help us* where children research people in the community who help keep them safe. Other stories that deal with strong versus weak would be useful reinforcement to this story, for example, *The Lion and the Mouse*, and *King Fox* in Cambridge Reading Adventures. These stories could be read aloud to the children.

Learning outcomes

Children can:

- read fluently with attention to punctuation
- discuss and interpret character and plot to support meaning.

A guided reading lesson

Introducing the text

Read the title and give each child a book.

Orientation

Give a brief orientation to the text: *In this story, a little boy meets a turtle who has swum all the way to the beach. At first the boy only notices how different Turtle looks – but maybe they could be friends. Let's read it and see.*

Preparation

Page 2: Turtle swims all the way to the beach. Where do you think he normally swims? In the story, the sea is called deep and green. Can you find the part where it says 'the deep green sea'?

Page 4: Does Turtle make a hole in the sand? Can you find the part that will tell us if we are right?

Page 8: The little boy thinks that Turtle is a dinosaur – why might he think that (drawing out the description of the turtle having wrinkly skin, feet with claws, beaked nose etc.)

Page 10 and 11: Turtle is made for living in the sea. But the boy isn't – he says that if he lived in the sea he would 'look just like an old man'. Find that part so we can practise it.

Page 12 and 13: The little boy runs off to play with his friends. He seems to be in trouble – who will come and help him?